W9-AEA-349

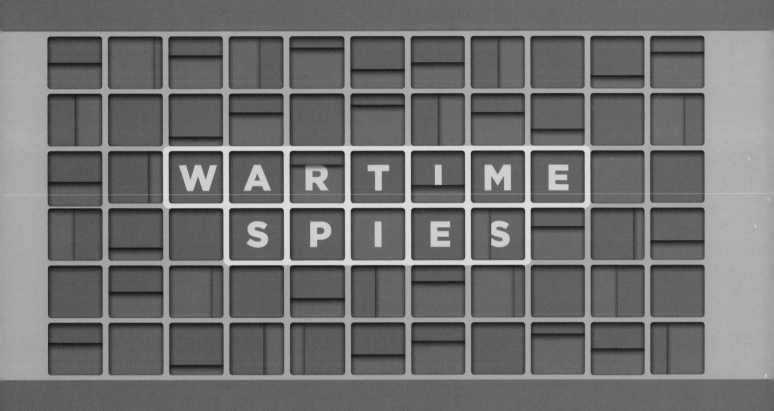

WARTIME SPIES

CREATIVE EDUCATION • CREATIVE PAPERBACKS

WORLD
WAR II SPIES

MICHAEL E. GOODMAN

Published by Creative Education and Creative Paperbacks
P.O. Box 227, Mankato, Minnesota 56002
Creative Education and Creative Paperbacks are imprints of
The Creative Company
www.thecreativecompany.us

Design and production by Chelsey Luther
Art direction by Rita Marshall
Printed in Malaysia

Photographs by AP Images (ASSOCIATED PRESS), Corbis (AP,
Berliner Verlag/Archiv/dpa, Bettmann, CORBIS, Hulton-Deutsch
Collection, John Springer Collection, Kingendai/AFLO/Nippon
News, Royal Mail/Splash News), Dreamstime (Georgesixth), Getty
Images (Barcroft Media, Bletchley Park Trust, CBS Photo Archive,
Keystone/Stringer, LAPI, Time Life Pictures), Lost & Taken (Brant
Wilson), Naval History and Heritage Command (Naval History and
Heritage Command/U.S. Navy), Newscom (akg-images, Digital
Press Photos, Everett Collection, Mirrorpix), Shutterstock (Patryk
Kosmider), SuperStock (Universal Images Group), TextureX.com
(TextureX), VectorTemplates.com

Library of Congress Cataloging-in-Publication Data
Goodman, Michael E.
World War II spies / Michael E. Goodman.
p. cm. — (Wartime spies)
Summary: A historical account of espionage during World War II,
including famous spies such as Eddie Chapman, covert missions,
and technologies that influenced the course of the conflict.
Includes bibliographical references and index.
ISBN 978-1-60818-603-7 (hardcover)
ISBN 978-1-62832-208-8 (pbk)
1. World War, 1939-1945—Secret service—Juvenile literature. 2.
Espionage—History—20th century—Juvenile literature. I. Title. II.
Title: World War Two spies.

D810.S7G64 2015
940.54'85—dc23   2014037536

CCSS: RI.5.1, 2, 3, 5, 6, 8; RH.6-8.3, 4, 5, 6, 7, 8, 9

First Edition HC 9 8 7 6 5 4 3 2 1
First Edition PBK 9 8 7 6 5 4 3 2 1

CONTENTS

CASUS BELLI

A Clever Clue   7

Economic and Political Unrest   8

CHAPTERS

CH. 1   Fighting against Might   10

CH. 2   Deceiving the Enemy   18

CH. 3   Courageous Women Operate Undercover   26

CH. 4   The 3 Cs   34

AT WAR'S END

A Violent Ending   42

COVERT OPS

The Big Secret   9

Germany's Traitorous Spymaster   13

Triple-Cross?   23

Making a City Move   29

Gangster Spies   39

Mind Games   43

World War II Timeline   44

Glossary   46

Selected Bibliography   47

Websites   47

Index   48

A CLEVER CLUE

In early 1943, *Allied* forces were planning to invade somewhere in southern Europe and begin an attack against German troops controlling much of the continent. The Germans expected an invasion but didn't know where it would take place. Then, on May 4, the Germans received a surprise. The body of a drowned British naval officer washed up on the coast of Spain, with a briefcase strapped to the body. Inside the case were plans detailing an Allied invasion scheduled for later that summer in Greece. A German *intelligence* officer rushed the information to *dictator* Adolf Hitler, who ordered his generals to send a large force to Greece to counter the attack. An invasion did begin on July 9, but it was at Sicily, nearly 500 miles (805 km) west of Greece. The body and the briefcase had been planted by Allied spies to trick the Germans. The deception worked and signaled a turning point in World War II.

ECONOMIC *and* POLITICAL UNREST

AFTER WORLD WAR I ended combat operations in 1918, dramatic economic and political changes began taking place around the world. Starting in the early 1930s, many countries experienced the *Great Depression*. Banks failed, people lost jobs, and most governments focused on economic problems. On the political front, several other countries began building empires. In Italy, a *Fascist* government under Benito Mussolini took control and later attacked Ethiopia and Libya in northern Africa. In the Far East, Japan invaded Manchuria and China.

All these developments made government leaders around the world nervous. However, the most disturbing activities were happening in Germany. Upon signing the Treaty of Versailles at the end of World War I, Germany was required to give up land, make payments to other countries for damages caused during the war, and disband most of

Germany's military and other forces were on display at each annual rally (1923–38) of the Nazi Party.

its military. Many Germans were angered and humiliated by these terms. They became even more upset when the German economy collapsed. In the midst of this unrest, Adolf Hitler gained popularity as he blamed Germany's problems on its Jewish citizens, and his National Socialist, or Nazi, Party took control of the government. Hitler began rebuilding Germany's military might, at first behind the scenes and then in plain sight of other nations. Other major Western powers—Great Britain, France, and the United States—were too preoccupied with their own economic problems or too tired of warfare to stop Germany as it took over the neighboring countries of Austria and Czechoslovakia. Hitler didn't stop there. He made alliances with Japan and Italy, forming what became known as the "Axis Powers," and made a separate "non-aggression" pact with the Soviet Union (as Russia was then known), agreeing that neither country would attack the other. Then, on September 1, 1939, Hitler's army and air force invaded Poland with a lightning-fast attack called a *blitzkrieg*. Shocked and worried for their own countries' safety, Great Britain and France declared war on Germany two days later, and World War II officially began.

COVERT OPS
THE BIG SECRET

Imagine asking 10,000 people to keep a secret. That's what the British government did with the more than 10,000 people who worked at Bletchley Park or in other parts of Britain and Europe. The codebreakers included engineers, mathematicians, translators, speed-writing specialists, radio operators, and puzzle experts. Some served in the military; others were civilians. Thousands of them spent hours each day listening in on radio traffic coming out of Germany and writing down each letter or number they detected. Then code experts, using early computers, **deciphered** the messages and determined their meaning. Amazingly, the whole operation was kept hush-hush—especially from the Germans.

CHAPTER ONE
FIGHTING *against* MIGHT

THERE IS AN OLD saying that "Might makes right." This means that the strongest opponent usually wins and gets its way. When World War II broke out in 1939, Germany had a stronger army and air force than any other nation in Europe, and its navy was growing. In the Pacific, Japan was far stronger than any of its neighbors and intent on using its powerful navy and air force to dominate the region. The U.S. could rival Germany's or Japan's military strength, but it was determined to stay out of the war at first. (The U.S. would eventually declare war against the Axis Powers in December 1941, following a surprise attack by the Japanese on the American naval base at Hawaii's Pearl Harbor.) Based on the idea of "might makes right," Germany and Japan were certain to win the war and control their parts of the world.

In fact, that is what was happening in 1939 and 1940. Pushing east, German forces quickly subdued Poland's inferior military. Then, turning west, they occupied the Netherlands, Belgium, Luxembourg, and large parts of France. To the north, Germany took control in Norway and Denmark and then moved southward into Greece and Yugoslavia. Meanwhile, the Japanese were spreading their empire

Japan used its fighter planes (opposite) in the East, while Germany bombed England (above).

over Korea, China, Indochina, and several island groups in the Pacific.

With the U.S. still on the sidelines, most of Europe looked to Great Britain and its newly elected prime minister Winston Churchill for leadership and direction. Taking office in May 1940, Churchill quickly recognized that the Axis Powers could not be stopped militarily at first. Instead, turning the tide would require a three-part strategy of espionage, deception, and *resistance*. By discovering their enemies' plans and undermining them, the other Western nations (known as the "Allies") might gain the edge. Undercover activities such as spying, trickery, and listening in on enemy communications would become keys to Allied victory in World War II.

Britain already had two professional espionage agencies known as MI5 and MI6. ("MI" stood for "Military Intelligence.") MI5 was in charge of counterespionage, or finding and stopping spies inside the country; MI6 was responsible for intelligence work outside Britain. Two other important espionage groups active during the war years were the Government Code and Cypher School (GC&CS) and the Double Cross Committee. The GC&CS (often referred to as "Bletchley Park" for the mansion outside London where it was based) was tasked with breaking codes and *ciphers* used by the Axis Powers for their military or government communications. Overseen by MI5, the Double

German soldiers had portable Enigma machines so that they could encode messages in the field.

Cross Committee—also known as the Twenty Committee because the Roman numerals for 20 (XX) form double crosses—was given the job of finding German spies working inside Britain and either arresting or "turning" them to become Allied *double agents*.

Both Bletchley Park and the Double Cross Committee were very successful. Throughout the war, the Germans used a complex cipher machine called Enigma to write their messages in code. The Germans believed their system was unbreakable, but they were wrong. Before the war, a group of engineers working within the Polish Cipher Bureau had stolen and studied an early version of Enigma. These

GERMANY'S TRAITOROUS SPYMASTER

Germany's spy service, the Abwehr, was not very effective during World War II. Perhaps it was no coincidence that the head of the Abwehr, Admiral Wilhelm Canaris, detested Adolf Hitler. Early in the war, Canaris gave minor intelligence roles to hundreds of untrained women and sent them to Britain. Many of the women were Jews whom Canaris helped escape death at the hands of the Nazis. He also leaked information about Nazi plans in Africa and Russia to the Allies. In 1944, Canaris was part of a group that planned an attempt on Hitler's life. He was caught and executed as a traitor.

Canaris (seated, middle) joined the German navy as a 17-year-old, commanding U-boats in World War I.

Enigma-encoded messages from the German army and air force were received in Bletchley's "registration room."

engineers helped the staff at Bletchley Park, who, by 1941, were able to understand most German communications. The intelligence reports that Bletchley Park provided to Allied leaders based on the deciphered messages were given their own code name—"Ultra"—because keeping them secret was ultra-important. The secret never was revealed. Hitler and other German leaders continued to use Enigma codes throughout the war, and the Allies were often able to anticipate and repel enemy attacks mentioned in the coded messages. "It was thanks to Ultra that we won the war," Churchill once remarked.

The Double Cross Committee also did its part to undermine the Germans. Before the start of the war, Hitler attempted to plant numerous spies inside Britain or to convince Germans already living there to become spies. Double Cross *operatives* identified and captured nearly every German agent in Great Britain. Most were imprisoned, while 13 were executed and 40 others agreed to work for the Allies. The double agents were used to provide *disinformation* that helped confuse and misdirect the Germans throughout the war.

Resistance was another core element of the Allies' plan for victory. With German troops occupying many countries in Western Europe and using strong-arm tactics to control residents, many Europeans felt powerless and angry. They wanted to fight back against the Nazis but feared deadly re-

Resistance groups often targeted railways—sometimes with dynamite or by removing bolts in tracks.

taliation. Some brave individuals in each country formed undercover groups to carry out sabotage operations. Sabotage included blowing up trains filled with soldiers and supplies, destroying bridges to slow down troop movements, and destroying factories producing weapons and war-related products. Other resistance efforts involved hiding soldiers and airmen trapped behind enemy lines and smuggling them to safety.

In July 1940, Churchill thought up a way to assist these resistance groups. He appointed Hugh Dalton, one of his government ministers, to create a new force of volunteers called the Special Operations Executive (SOE). The SOE recruited and trained civilian operatives in England and then slipped them into occupied countries by parachute, ship, or train. The agents had varied backgrounds and came from many different countries—including the U.S., despite its official *neutral* stance at the time. The volunteers learned how to land safely by parachute, how to disguise themselves, how to encode and transmit messages, how to plant explosives, how to escape from handcuffs, and even how to kill an enemy with their bare hands. Once inside enemy territory, SOE agents trained resistance fighters and made sure supplies arrived for their covert, or hidden, operations. They also radioed spy reports on enemy troop numbers and movements.

Being an SOE agent was dangerous work, and punishment for those captured in occupied countries was usually swift and harsh. Many of the most active SOE agents were women. In previous wars, women caught spying were often given warnings or light punishments, but that was not true in World War II. A high percentage of women SOE agents were captured, and many of them were executed.

Great care was taken before an SOE agent was sent behind enemy lines. Their clothing and possessions had to be right for the area to which they were sent. Even their dental work sometimes had to be altered to look like a French or Dutch dentist had done it. Agents were searched before they got on a plane to make sure they were not carrying any items that might give them away, such as gum, matches, or photos from home.

Once the Americans entered the war, a new group of operatives began working in Europe and in the Pacific to assist resistance efforts and spy on the enemy. They were part of a new intelligence agency called the Office of Strategic Services (OSS), formed under the direction of president Franklin D. Roosevelt in 1942. (The OSS was the forerunner of the Central Intelligence Agency [CIA] that still oversees spying for the U.S.) OSS operatives gathered intelligence needed by Allied army and navy units, smuggled supplies to resistance groups, and even recruited locals in Europe and on Pacific islands to be spies.

By 1944, Americans in Britain were receiving instruction from the OSS on demolitions tactics.

CHAPTER TWO
DECEIVING *the* ENEMY

ESPIONAGE AND RESISTANCE WERE two parts of Churchill's plan for defeating the Axis Powers. The third key element was deception. Some of the most amazing Allied victories in the war were the result of clever deceptions, brilliant intelligence work, and careful planning. Here are three examples:

In June 1942, six months after Pearl Harbor, the Japanese planned a major offensive, or attack, to drive the U.S. out of the Pacific islands. They intended to surprise and destroy the American fleet near the Midway Atoll, 1,300 miles (2,092 km) west of Hawaii. American code-breakers decrypted messages about a potential battle site identified by the letters *AF*. Admiral Chester Nimitz, the commander in chief of the U.S. Pacific Fleet, suspected that "AF" was a code name for Midway, but to be sure, he put out a fake report that water supplies at the American base on Midway were contaminated. Almost immediately, Japanese communications carried a report that fresh water was a problem on AF and even discussed the proposed date for the surprise offensive. Now sure of the place and time for the Japanese attack, Nimitz set his forces into battle positions. The Japanese attacked but were soundly defeated. The Battle of Midway was a major

General Douglas MacArthur and Admiral Nimitz (left to right) strategized battle plans in the Pacific (opposite).

The 1,100 members of the American "Ghost Army" utilized inflatable tanks and other trickery in France.

setback for the Japanese, derailing plans to dominate the Pacific.

In 1943 and 1944, two deception plans known as Operation Barclay and Operation Bodyguard played key roles in the Allies' plan to move forces onto the European continent and defeat the Nazis. You read about a portion of Operation Barclay known as "Mincemeat" in the introduction to this book. Operation Barclay was an overall plan to trick the Axis Powers into moving troops to Greece and leaving Sicily poorly defended—which would allow the Allies to invade southern Europe and begin driving the Nazis from countries they were occupying. The Mincemeat part

of the operation called for British intelligence leaders to obtain a dead body in England, preserve it, and then modify the body to look as if the man had drowned. The body was dressed in a British major's uniform and provided with identification cards and a briefcase containing plans for a Greek invasion. Then the corpse was placed in the Mediterranean Sea just off the coast of Spain. When it washed up on shore, German intelligence found the fake documents and alerted their generals to move their forces. The resulting successful Allied landing in Sicily (known as Operation Husky) helped pave the way for an ultimate Allied victory in Europe.

Operation Bodyguard was even more complicated than Barclay. It was a plan to deceive the Nazis into believing that the landing in northern France at Normandy on June 6, 1944 (known as "D-Day") was just a decoy, and the real Allied invasion was going to be made at Pas-de-Calais some 270 miles (435 km) farther northeast. As part of Operation Bodyguard, Allied leaders began sending out messages that discussed moving a million troops to the British coast, just across the English Channel from Pas-de-Calais. This disinformation was echoed in communications to Germany from double agents. Then engineers used rubber and cardboard to create hundreds of fake tanks and planes that looked real when viewed from a plane flying overhead. How well did Operation Bodyguard work? For weeks after the actual invasion at Normandy, the main body of German troops remained based near Pas-de-Calais anticipating the "real" Allied attack.

Omaha Beach was 1 of 5 sectors where troops landed along 50 miles (80.5 km) of Normandy coastline.

Big operations were important in the Allied victory, but creative and resourceful individuals also played key roles in deceiving the Axis Powers. Two of the most unusual and fascinating masters of deception were Spaniard Joan Pujol Garcia and British thief-turned-spy Eddie Chapman. Strangely, both men started out working as spies for Germany and switched their allegiance to Britain and the Allies.

Pujol never planned to be a German spy. In fact, he hated the Nazis for supporting his country's dictator, Francisco Franco. He wanted to do everything he could to topple Hitler's regime. He volunteered to be a spy for the British but was turned down. It is not clear why, but perhaps intelligence leaders didn't trust him. So Pujol conceived a new plan: he would offer to spy for the Germans, win their trust, and then turn himself into a double agent for the British.

The Nazis accepted Pujol, trained him in Germany, and then sent him to Britain to begin spying. Only he didn't actually go to Britain. He stopped off in Portugal (with permission from his trainers), pretended to fly from there to Britain, and sent false reports back to Germany from Portugal. How did he get away with this deception? He was a terrific actor, and the Germans were desperate to have a spy in Britain, since most of their original agents had been caught. Some of Pujol's early reports to Berlin were intercepted by Bletchley Park, where they aroused confusion because he was writing about events and places that didn't actually exist. Double Cross operatives found Pujol, set him up as a double agent, and gave him the code name "Garbo," after famous Hollywood actress Greta Garbo. While still living secretly in Portugal, Garbo invented a ring of more than 20 imaginary agents who continued to provide disinformation to Germany. In 1943, Garbo was instructed to file real intelligence to the Nazis concerning an Allied invasion in North Africa, but the information was timed to arrive in German hands too late to be useful. Still, Hitler was so impressed with his spy's accurate report that he awarded him a medal for outstanding service. Later,

Francisco Franco (right) sought Spanish inclusion in the Axis Powers, but Hitler denied his demands.

TRIPLE-CROSS?

Parisian-born Mathilde Carré wanted to be a spy. She just couldn't decide which side she should support. In 1940, she fell in love with a Polish pilot working for the French Resistance and joined him in his undercover work. When she and her boyfriend were captured by the Germans in November 1941, she agreed to become a German double agent to save herself. A few months later, she infiltrated a British intelligence unit, but one of the unit's leaders accused her of working for the Germans. Bursting into tears, she offered to become a triple agent. Instead, she was arrested and jailed.

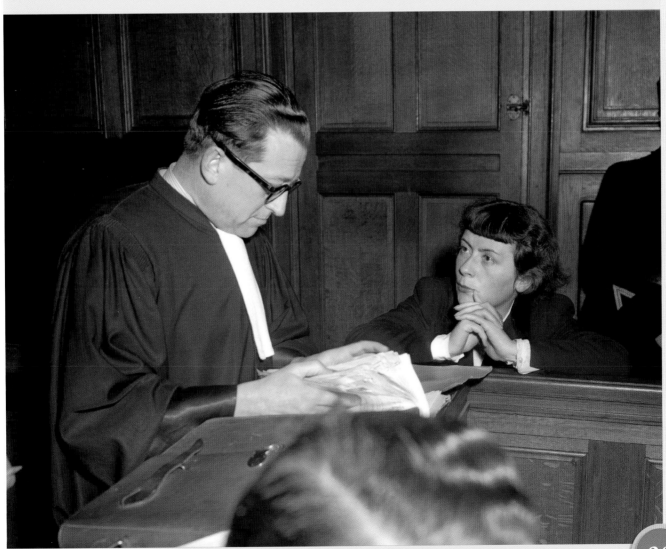

After a 1949 trial, Carré was sentenced to death but served a five-year prison term instead.

Garbo would provide fake reports that helped support the scheme behind Operation Bodyguard.

Chapman proved to be a better double agent than bank robber. When the war began, he was in prison on the British island of Jersey, located near France. After German troops occupied Jersey, Chapman decided his best bet for getting out of jail was to volunteer to be a German spy. He convinced the Nazi commander that he hated Britain and could be bribed to be a traitor to his country. In December 1942, Chapman, using the German code name "Fritz," was parachuted into England and given a radio, pistol, cyanide suicide capsule, and 1,000 British pounds (worth about $68,000 today). He walked into the nearest town and turned himself in to British authorities, who contacted the Double Cross Committee.

Chapman soon received an assignment from his German *spymasters* to blow up an aircraft factory near London. Double Cross agents knew that by carrying out the assignment, Chapman could earn the Nazis' trust, but were the British really willing to sacrifice a valuable war factory to make a double agent look good? Luckily, they came up with a solution. One key member of Britain's spy team was a professional magician named Jasper Maskelyne. He began work on an illusion to fool the Nazis. Maskelyne and his "Magic Gang" sewed together a giant canvas cover for the factory's roof. Then they painted the canvas to look as if the roof had large holes in it through which damaged factory parts could be seen by German *reconnaissance* planes flying overhead. They also made papier mâché models of engine parts, bricks, and equipment to scatter outside the "destroyed" plant. The trick worked. The Germans were very pleased with Fritz's spy work, and he continued to deceive his Nazi bosses for two more years. After the war, Great Britain granted Chapman a prison pardon for his service to his country.

The Fw 189 Uhu was a German recon aircraft known for its twin beam-like housings called booms.

CHAPTER THREE

COURAGEOUS WOMEN OPERATE UNDERCOVER

WOMEN PLAYED IMPORTANT ESPIONAGE roles during World War II and were especially effective as undercover agents. In World War II, unlike in earlier wars, female spies sometimes fired guns, planted explosives, and broke into enemy safes. Key Allied female operatives were seldom called by their real names by friends or enemies. Instead, they were known by code names such as "the White Mouse," "the Limping Lady," and "Hedgehog." In addition to the hundreds of regular, everyday women, a princess, a famous Parisian entertainer, and several other celebrities worked undercover to help the Allied cause.

"The White Mouse" was a New Zealander named Nancy Wake, who was living with her husband in France when the Germans invaded in 1940. Her undercover career began one day when she noticed a young man in a Paris café reading an English book. After learning that the man was a British pilot stranded in France, she and her husband helped sneak him to safety across the Spanish border. Wake next fixed up an old ambulance and began smuggling more Allied soldiers to safety. Then she became involved in other espionage activities. Soon, the Nazis were hunting the spy they called "the White Mouse"

While Nancy Wake (above) helped the French, other women fought with the Yugoslav Partisans (opposite).

because of her ability to elude capture. The Germans even offered a 5-million-franc reward for her arrest. Wake escaped to Britain, where she was trained in sabotage by the SOE and impressed her instructors with her ability to shoot quickly and accurately. She returned to France in April 1944 and helped turn a French Resistance group into an effective fighting force of more than 7,000 men and women. Many years after the war, Wake wrote a book about her wartime adventures.

Like Wake, Virginia Hall served with the SOE in France. She later switched to the OSS after the U.S. entered the war and became a valuable radio operator and intelligence gatherer in occupied France. Hall came from a prominent family in Baltimore, Maryland, and studied abroad for college. She became fluent in French, German, and Italian—which she put to use during her spying missions. After the war broke out, Hall joined the SOE. Using the *cover* of an American newspaper reporter, Hall did double duty: she reported to American readers how badly German soldiers were treating French civilians, and she helped smuggle downed American airmen and prisoners of war out of France. In some of her news reports, she would embed secret intelligence concerning German troop numbers and movements.

Like Wake, Hall received a nickname from the Germans, who tried unsuccessfully to capture her. She was called "the Limping Lady" because she had an artificial leg—the result of a hunting accident earlier in her life. Despite her limp, Hall carried out some amazing operations that earned her the respect of her fellow spies and the hatred of the Gestapo, the German secret police. A Gestapo poster was once circulated throughout France with Hall's portrait and this ominous message: "The woman who limps is one of the most valuable Allied agents in France, and we must find and destroy her." Luckily, the Germans never caught her. After the war, U.S. president Harry S. Truman planned to award Hall the Distinguished Service Cross at a public ceremony. She said she would accept the medal only if it was presented to her in private, because she wanted to remain undercover as a member of the newly formed CIA.

The spy known as "Hedgehog" was born Marie-Madeleine Bridou in Marseille in southern France. She joined the French Resistance in 1940. The next year, the leader of her resistance group suggested that she form her own spy network to report on German troop movements. "But I'm only

COVERT OPS
MAKING A CITY MOVE

In 1941, British army Major Jasper Maskelyne formed a camouflage unit in North Africa. Its most daring deception involved making the Egyptian city of Alexandria "move." Allied leaders learned the Germans were planning a late-night bombing raid on Alexandria's harbor to disrupt Allied shipping in the area. So Maskelyne's "Magic Gang" built a mock-up of the harbor, complete with lights and dummy ships and submarines, three miles (4.8 km) away. When German bombers carried out their plan, Maskelyne had the real lights of the city turned off and his new lights on. The German planes fell for the trick and dropped their bombs harmlessly on the phony harbor.

Many of Maskelyne's purported wartime disappearing acts may have been pure invention themselves.

a woman," she reportedly said. "Right," she was told, "and who would suspect a woman of being such an excellent spy?" Bridou began assembling her network, which she called "the Alliance," and assigned members code names based on animal species. For example, one very tall member was called "Giraffe." Bridou chose "Hedgehog" for herself. The Gestapo soon became aware of the group's existence and gave it a code name of its own—"Noah's Ark." Bridou kept recruiting new members and, at one time, was directing 3,000 undercover agents. The information they reported to Britain was vital to Allied efforts to break the Germans' stranglehold on Western Europe.

Eventually, the Gestapo began hunting down Noah's Ark members with the help of a *mole* who had infiltrated the group. Bridou and several others were arrested. Bridou managed to escape and resume her spy work. In 1943, British intelligence flew her to safety in England, where she continued to direct Noah's Ark. She returned to France after D-Day but was soon captured again. This time, she made a daring escape by taking off her clothes and edging her thin body between the bars of her cell. Many other members of Bridou's Alliance were not so lucky. After the war, Bridou learned that 438 of her agents had been executed as spies.

One spy who had a royal background was Noor Inayat Khan, the descendant of an Indian sultan. Khan, who was living in Paris when the Germans invaded in 1940, fled to London, where she joined the SOE. After her training was complete, she was flown back to France in July 1943 to become a radio operator for a resistance group operating inside Paris. When several members of Khan's group were captured, her SOE bosses urged her to return to London. However, she insisted on staying to continue transmitting intelligence about enemy activities. Khan eluded capture by the Gestapo for many months by biking, with transmitter in tow, to a different "safe house" each day. She was finally caught and thrown into prison. After several attempts to

A bronze bust of Khan was dedicated in 2012 by Anne, the Princess Royal, in Gordon Square Garden.

Established in 1933 as the first Nazi concentration camp, Dachau served as the model for the others.

escape, Khan was transferred to the Dachau concentration camp in Germany, where she faced death by firing squad. Today, a statue in London honors her bravery.

While the Nazis in Paris were hunting for the Hedgehog and the princess, they never suspected that famed singer and dancer Josephine Baker was also an Allied spy. Baker, an African American

originally from St. Louis, Missouri, had moved to Paris years before and had become a sensation in her new home. Even after the Nazis occupied France, she was often invited to parties attended by German officers and politicians. She mingled with the guests, who were happy to converse with a famous star. Sometimes they blurted out secrets that Baker would write down in invisible ink on pages of her sheet music and convey to Resistance leaders. One time, she even managed to snatch a copy of a German-Italian codebook that she passed along. Baker continued to perform and to gather intelligence throughout the war years. She also donated much of the money she earned to support the French Resistance.

Baker was not the only woman celebrity doing espionage work during World War II. Future world-renowned chef Julia Child was recruited into the OSS. She helped develop a repellent to keep sharks from setting off underwater explosives the OSS used to blow up German submarines. Some people even believe that famed pilot Amelia Earhart may have been flying a reconnaissance mission over Pacific islands occupied by the Japanese when her plane disappeared in June 1937, several years before the attack on Pearl Harbor. The rumors have never been proven.

When British troops had a break from fighting, they enjoyed attending performances by Baker.

CHAPTER FOUR
THE 3 Cs

MUCH OF THE ESPIONAGE activity afoot during World War II was coordinated by organizations such as the SOE, OSS, Abwehr, Noah's Ark, and MI6. Yet some individual spies worked mostly alone and stood out for their courage, commitment, and concentration—"the 3 Cs" of spying.

A good example of someone who possessed the 3 Cs was Japanese naval officer Takeo Yoshikawa, who arrived in Hawaii in March 1941 posing as a member of the Japanese *embassy* staff. His orders were simple: move around the islands and learn all he could about how they were guarded by the American navy. He was to pay special attention to the movements of ships at the American base at Pearl Harbor and planes patrolling the waters around Hawaii. He was also warned by his *handler*, "Don't make yourself conspicuous; maintain a normal, business-as-usual attitude; keep calm under all circumstances; avoid taking risks; and, above all, don't get caught."

For the next six months, Yoshikawa, who spoke English well, followed his orders carefully. Many days, he would go for a picnic on a hillside overlooking Pearl Harbor and watch the boats and the planes. He noted the direction the planes usually flew when they left the

After Yoshikawa's intel led to the Pearl Harbor attack, the USS Indianapolis *(left) looked for the Japanese.*

Centrally located in Pearl Harbor, Ford Island's naval air station was a prime target to attack.

base and determined on which day of the week the most ships remained at anchor in the harbor. He let his handler know the answers: the planes generally flew toward the south, and the day with the greatest number of ships in the harbor was Sunday. Yoshikawa put his findings into coded messages that he transmitted to Tokyo. (Amazingly, some of these messages were intercepted and decoded by American intelligence, but no one paid much attention to them.)

On Saturday evening, December 6, 1941, Yoshikawa coded his final message and waited for the attack he thought might be coming the next morning. He was right. Japanese bombers arrived from the north the morning of Sunday, December 7, and destroyed much of the American fleet in Pearl Harbor. As the bombers struck, Yoshikawa rushed to the embassy, where he helped burn top-secret papers and codebooks. He was arrested and brought back to the U.S. for questioning. He returned home in August 1942 as part of a prisoner exchange. Back in Japan, Yoshikawa was given no medals or special recognition. He was simply a lonely spy who had done his job well.

Richard Sakakida also did spy work in the Pacific but had a very different background from Yoshikawa's. He was born in Hawaii to Japanese parents and was fluent in both English and Japanese. In early 1941, Sakakida was recruited by U.S. Army intelligence to go undercover in the Philippines and blend in with Japanese people living there. He developed friendships with Japanese businessmen on the islands and used those connections to learn details about Japan's plans in the Pacific. After the Pearl Harbor attack, the Japanese began landing forces in the Philippines, and Sakakida was ordered to evacuate to Australia. Instead, he offered his spot on the evacuation plane to a civilian agent who had a family to protect.

Sakakida was eventually captured and taken to a prison camp, where he was tortured for five months. He kept insisting that he was a civilian working with the local Japanese businessmen, and his captors finally believed him. They assigned him to act as an interpreter for a Japanese colonel interrogating other American prisoners. Sometimes the prisoners would make insulting comments to the colonel, but Sakakida would provide a "soft" translation that helped them avoid extra punishment. Sakakida also read and memorized classified materials on the colonel's desk and passed the in-

Filipino and American prisoners of the Japanese suffered and died as they were forcibly relocated in 1942.

formation along to resistance group leaders who were hiding near the prison camp. The information helped American forces make successful air attacks on the Philippines. Later, Sakakida helped engineer a prison break by masquerading as a Japanese officer and barking commands to the prison guards in very official-sounding Japanese. More than 500 men escaped and fled into the mountains.

Later, Sakakida escaped and joined a group of *guerillas* based in the mountains, where he was badly wounded in a raid. Somehow he managed to survive and was finally rescued in September 1945 by American forces liberating the Philippines. After the war, both the Filipino and American governments honored Sakakida with awards.

In Norway, on the other side of the world from where Yoshikawa and Sakakida did their spying, resistance fighter Gunnar Sonsteby was carrying out missions against the German army occupying his home country. He operated under the code name "Kjakan" ("the Chin"). Among his many espionage skills, Sonsteby was a master forger. He was able to duplicate perfectly the Nazi police chief's signature and forged numerous identity cards that he and others used to move safely around Nazi-controlled Norway between 1940 and 1945.

In 1944, Sonsteby organized "the Oslo Gang," a group of saboteurs who made life difficult for the Nazis. The Gang played an important role after D-Day by damaging rail lines used by German troops and by sinking a German transport ship carrying troops and supplies toward the front lines in France. They also bombed a recruitment office in Oslo, which prevented the Nazis from drafting young Norwegians into the German army.

After the war, Sonsteby was asked to join both the Norwegian and British intelligence services. He declined. "I don't want any more war," he explained. "I have lost five years of my life to war."

Polish-born Krystyna Skarbek's bravery, toughness, and determination demonstrated the 3 Cs. Like Sonsteby, she was determined to fight back against German

When Skarbek became a British citizen in 1946, she adopted her code name of Christine Granville.

GANGSTER SPIES

In 1943, Charles "Lucky" Luciano, the head of organized crime in the U.S., was serving a long sentence in a New York prison. Luciano happened to have strong criminal connections on the Italian island of Sicily, where the Allies were planning an invasion. OSS leaders met with Luciano and asked him to contact mobsters in Sicily for assistance before and during the invasion. Luciano then enlisted the help of Calogero Vizzini, Sicily's crime boss. Vizzini's men patrolled roads near the invasion site, keeping German snipers away and helping ensure the invasion's success. For his help, Luciano was granted early release after the war and deported to Italy.

Known as the original "boss" of what became the Genovese crime family, Luciano was born in Sicily.

troops occupying her country. Using the code name "Christine Granville," she carried out some of the most daring spy missions of the war. Several of her fellow operatives jokingly called her "Willing," because she was ready to face any danger.

Moving across the border to Hungary, Granville spent the first part of the war carrying messages to and from members of the Polish underground and helping stranded Polish soldiers escape. These missions required her to cross the steep Tatra Mountains in southern Poland many times, often on skis. On one of her trips, she was carrying secret documents and a large sum of money when she was stopped by German guards. She managed to throw away the documents before being searched but had no good explanation for the money. She simply offered the money to the guards if they would let her go, and they took it.

Later in the war, she worked with the SOE in southern France, carrying vital messages and supplies to resistance groups. She had two items—a razor-sharp commando knife and a cyanide suicide capsule—sewn inside her skirt, just in case she was caught during one of these missions. Luckily, she never needed to use either, but she often had to employ quick thinking. One time, the leader of her SOE group and two other captured agents were being held in a Gestapo jail awaiting execution. Granville stormed into the prison, shouting that she was the niece of an Allied general whose forces were marching toward the jail. She informed the two Frenchmen in charge that they would surely be hanged by the Allies if they didn't let the prisoners go. The frightened jailers handed over the spies and rushed to escape themselves. Once again, "Willing" had been willing to risk her life for her mission, and once more, she had survived.

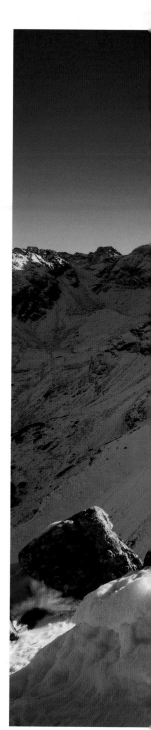

Even the highest range in the Carpathian Mountains, the Tatras, was no obstacle to Skarbek.

A VIOLENT ENDING

WORLD WAR II BEGAN in a blaze of violence whenever it struck a new theater, or area—from the 1939 German blitzkrieg of Poland to the 1941 attack on Pearl Harbor. Other violent acts contributed to its end, both in Europe and in the Pacific. On April 30, 1945, Adolf Hitler, realizing that his hopes to establish a German empire were shattered, retreated to a bunker beneath his headquarters in Berlin. There he swallowed a cyanide capsule and then shot himself in the head. Nine days later, Germany agreed to surrender to the Allies, bringing an end to the war in Europe.

Fighting would continue in the Pacific for several more months. Then American president Harry Truman made a momentous decision. Truman's political and military advisers felt

"The bombs ... made it wholly clear that we must never have another war," said U.S. official Henry Stimson.

strongly that the Japanese would fight "to the death" if the Allies attacked their homeland and that those battles might cost millions of additional lives. Therefore, Truman ordered his military leaders to drop an atomic bomb on the city of Hiroshima. No such weapon had ever been used in wartime, and no one knew just what damage the bomb could cause to civilians and property. But Truman and his advisers reasoned that the costs of not using the bomb outweighed the potential damages. The bomb was dropped on August 6. When the Japanese failed to surrender within three days, a second bomb was detonated on the city of Nagasaki. The damage caused by the two bombs was remarkable—between 100,000 and 120,000 died instantly (mostly from burns), and more than 70,000 additional deaths resulted from the long-term effects of radiation generated by the bombs. Japanese leaders reluctantly surrendered.

Both the German and Japanese dreams of empire ended in destruction, and a second 20th-century war that had engulfed almost the entire world was finally over. Soldiers and spies who had survived the war returned home to begin the healing process.

COVERT OPS
MIND GAMES

During World War II, the Germans and Japanese used radio *propaganda* broadcasts to try to upset Allied servicemen and convince them to give up. Two of the most famous broadcasters were Mildred Gillars (known as "Axis Sally") and Iva Toguri D'Aquino (known as "Tokyo Rose"). Both women were American-born and spoke perfect English. Gillars's messages predicting Allied defeat in Europe were beamed out from Berlin nightly from December 1941 until May 1945. D'Aquino's Pacific broadcasts regularly teased American sailors that their sweethearts back home were being unfaithful. The propaganda was ultimately ineffective, and both women were convicted of treason after the war.

WORLD WAR II
TIMELINE

OCTOBER– NOVEMBER 1936	Germany signs pacts with Italy and Japan, forming the Axis Powers.
JULY 7, 1937	Japan invades China, starting World War II in the Pacific.
SEPTEMBER 29, 1938	Germany, Italy, Great Britain, and France sign the Munich Agreement allowing Germany to expand its territory without objection.
AUGUST 23, 1939	Nazi Germany and the Soviet Union sign an agreement not to attack each other.
SEPTEMBER 1–3, 1939	Germany invades Poland; Great Britain and France declare war on Germany.
MAY–JUNE 1940	Germany attacks and occupies France, Belgium, Luxembourg, and the Netherlands.
JUNE 1940	Italy enters the war and invades southern France.
JULY 10, 1940– OCTOBER 31, 1940	German planes attack England in the unsuccessful Battle of Britain.
JUNE 1941	Germany invades the Soviet Union.
DECEMBER 7, 1941	Japan bombs Pearl Harbor; the United States declares war on Japan.

JUNE 4–7, 1942	The Allies defeat Japan in the Battle of Midway.
MAY 12, 1943	Axis troops in North Africa surrender.
JULY 9, 1943	The Allies invade southern Europe at Sicily.
SEPTEMBER 8, 1943	Italy surrenders to the Allies.
JUNE 6, 1944 (D-DAY)	Allied troops land in France and begin invasion of occupied Europe.
DECEMBER 16, 1944– JANUARY 25, 1945	Germany wages an offensive campaign called the Battle of the Bulge on the Western Front.
APRIL 30, 1945	Hitler commits suicide.
MAY 8, 1945	Germany surrenders, ending World War II in Europe.
AUGUST 6 AND 9, 1945	The U.S. drops atomic bombs on Hiroshima and Nagasaki.
SEPTEMBER 2, 1945	Japan signs a surrender agreement, officially ending the war.

GLOSSARY

ALLIED—connected with the nations fighting against Germany, Japan, and Italy during World War II

CIPHERS—messages composed in secret writing based on a key or set of symbols

COVER—the made-up occupation or purpose of an agent

DECIPHERED—converted a coded message, or cipher, into normal text

DICTATOR—a ruler with absolute power who often uses that power in a bullying way; a tyrant

DISINFORMATION—false or misleading intelligence, often provided by double agents or issued by an organization as propaganda

DOUBLE AGENTS—spies who pretend to work for one country or organization while acting on behalf of another

EMBASSY—the headquarters of an ambassador and staff in a foreign country

FASCIST—relating to the political party in Italy that set up a dictatorship before World War II

GREAT DEPRESSION—the period of terrible worldwide economic conditions that began in 1929 and lasted throughout most of the 1930s

GUERILLAS—groups of fighters, not part of an official army, who make surprise raids, often behind enemy lines

HANDLER—a person who trains or is responsible for spies working in a certain place

INTELLIGENCE—information of political or military value uncovered and transmitted by a spy

MOLE—an employee of one intelligence service who actually works for another service or who works undercover within the enemy group in order to gather intelligence

NEUTRAL—not taking sides in a conflict or argument

OPERATIVES—secret agents working for an intelligence group

PROPAGANDA—material distributed to promote a government's or group's point of view or to damage an opposing point of view; some propaganda is untrue or unfairly exaggerated

RECONNAISSANCE—scouting or exploring, often for a militaristic or strategic purpose

RESISTANCE—an organized underground movement or people fighting against a foreign power occupying their country

SPYMASTERS—people who recruit and are in charge of a group of spies

SELECTED BIBLIOGRAPHY

Atwood, Kathryn J. *Women Heroes of World War II: Twenty-six Stories of Espionage, Sabotage, Resistance, and Rescue.* Chicago: Chicago Review Press, 2011.

Breuer, William B. *Top Secret Tales of World War II.* New York: Wiley, 2000.

Janeczko, Paul B. *The Dark Game: True Spy Stories.* Somerville, Mass.: Candlewick, 2010.

McIntosh, Elizabeth P. *Sisterhood of Spies: The Women of the OSS.* Annapolis, Md.: Naval Institute, 1998.

Payment, Simone. *American Women Spies of World War II.* New York: Rosen, 2004.

Rosenberg, Tina. "D for Deception," in *The Atavist*, no. 16: August 2012.

Shapiro, Stephen, and Tina Forrester. *Ultra Hush-Hush: Espionage and Special Missions.* New York: Annick, 2003.

Sulick, Michael J. *Spying in America: Espionage from the Revolutionary War to the Dawn of the Cold War.* Washington, D.C.: Georgetown University Press, 2012.

WEBSITES

BBC HISTORY
http://www.bbc.co.uk/history/worldwars/wwtwo/
A collection of articles and videos, including a special section on "The Secret War" that focuses on important espionage operations and activities during World War II.

NATIONAL WOMEN'S HISTORY MUSEUM SPIES EXHIBITION
http://www.nwhm.org/online-exhibits/spies/2.htm
Brief biographies of notable women spies and descriptions of their espionage activities from the American Revolution to the Cold War.

INDEX

Africa 8, 13, 22, 29

Allied invasion of Sicily 7, 20, 39

   and Operation Barclay 20

Baker, Josephine 32–33

Battle of Midway 18

Bridou, Marie-Madeleine 28, 30

   and "Alliance" spy network 30

Canaris, Adm. Wilhelm 13

Carré, Mathilde 23

Chapman, Eddie 22, 24

Child, Julia 33

Churchill, Winston 12, 14, 15

coded messages 9, 12, 14, 36

   and Enigma machine 12, 14

     See also Great Britain: Bletchley Park codebreakers

counterespionage 12

cover stories 28

Dalton, Hugh 15

D-Day invasion of Normandy 20, 21, 22, 24, 30, 38

   and Operation Bodyguard 20, 21, 22, 24

double agents 12, 14, 21, 22, 24

France 9, 10, 21, 24, 26, 28, 30, 32, 38, 40

Franco, Francisco 22

Germany 7, 8–9, 10, 12, 13, 14, 20, 21, 22, 23, 24, 26, 28, 29, 30,
     32, 34, 38, 40, 42, 43

   Abwehr 13, 34

   concentration camps 32

   Gestapo 28, 30, 40

   and invasions of other nations 9, 10, 14, 26, 30, 38

   Nazis 9, 13, 14, 20, 22, 24, 26, 32, 38

   and Treaty of Versailles 8–9

Great Britain 9, 12, 13, 14, 15–16, 20, 22, 24, 28, 30, 34, 40

   Bletchley Park codebreakers 9, 12, 14, 22

   Double Cross Committee 12, 14, 22, 24

   GC&CS 12

   MI5 12

   MI6 12, 34

   SOE 15–16, 28, 30, 34, 40

Great Depression 8

Hall, Virginia 28

handlers 34, 36

Hitler, Adolf 7, 9, 13, 14, 22, 42

Italy 8, 9, 39

Japan 8, 9, 10, 12, 18, 33, 34, 36, 37, 38, 43

   and invasions of other nations 8, 12

Kahn, Noor Inayat 30, 32

Luciano, Charles "Lucky" 39

Maskelyne, Jasper 24, 29

moles 30

Mussolini, Benito 8

Nimitz, Adm. Chester 18

Philippines 37–38

propaganda 43

Pujol Garcia, Joan 22, 24

resistance efforts 15, 16, 23, 28, 30, 33, 38, 40

Roosevelt, Franklin D. 16

Russia 9, 13

Sakakida, Richard 37–38

Skarbek, Krystyna 38, 40

Sonsteby, Gunnar 38

spy tools 32, 38

spy tradecraft 15

Truman, Harry S. 28, 42–43

United States 9, 10, 12, 15, 16, 18, 28, 33, 34, 36,
     37, 39, 42, 43

   CIA 16, 28

   OSS 16, 28, 33, 34, 39

   Pearl Harbor attack 10, 18, 33, 36, 37, 42

   usage of atomic bombs 43

Wake, Nancy 26, 28

World War I 8

Yoshikawa, Takeo 34, 36, 37, 38

   spy work at Pearl Harbor 34, 36